FAITHWORKS: INTIMACY AND INVOLVEMENT

Other books in the series include:

Faithworks
Faithworks: Stories of Hope
Faithworks Unpacked
100 Proven Ways to Transform Your Community

FAITHWORKS
Intimacy and Involvement

STEVE CHALKE

WITH

SIMON JOHNSTON

KINGSWAY PUBLICATIONS
EASTBOURNE

First published 2003
Reprinted 2003

Unless otherwise indicated, biblical quotations are
from the New International Version © 1973, 1978, 1984
by the International Bible Society.

ISBN 1 84291 118 X

Published by
KINGSWAY COMMUNICATIONS LTD
Lottbridge Drove, Eastbourne BN23 6NT, England.
Email: books@kingsway.co.uk

Book design and production for the publishers by
Bookprint Creative Services, P.O. Box 827, BN21 3YJ, England.
Printed in Great Britain.

Contents

Acknowledgements   6

Foreword   7

1. Turning the Tide:
   Faithworks Spirituality   11

2. Intimacy and Involvement:
   Spirituality in the Old Testament   24

3. Intimacy and Involvement:
   Spirituality in the New Testament   40

4. How the West Was Lost:
   The Retreat of the Church   57

5. A Moment of Opportunity:
   The Role of the Church in the Twenty-first Century   69

6. The Faithworks Movement:
   How to Get Involved   81

7. The Faithworks Partners   90

Acknowledgements

Thanks to Liam and Katy Eaglestone, who somehow managed to find time in the week before their marriage to read the book and draw up the end-of-chapter questions; to Aredi Pitsiaeli, Gareth Wallace, Emily Chalke, Meic Pearse and Derek Tidball, who have each given the manuscript careful consideration and been forthcoming with their insights at various stages of the process; to Anthony Watkis for his exacting work on our grammar; to Alan Mann, whose theological contribution to the project has not only been considerable but invaluable; to Ani Wright for organizing us and to the whole Faithworks team for their dedication to the cause.

Foreword

The test of faith

Religion and politics – not in polite company. Together they were taboos to be restricted to private discussion. Perhaps this was because the two subjects were too important and would interrupt the small talk. Or maybe it was because they were potentially so divisive that they might spoil the party.

That common wisdom has changed over the years. Both politics and religion are hot topics these days. Many people today are searching for a spirituality in which to ground their lives and work. Others, who are part of religious communities, are asking how their faith might be connected to the urgent problems of their world. The coming years promise to deepen the relationship between faith and politics as the two are joined and proceed together.

The question now is putting faith – a prophetic spirituality – into action. We have to act on our faith, or it really doesn't mean anything. Real faith leads inevitably to transformation – both of individuals and societies. A prophetic faith can speak to the hunger among us for personal and social change. It leads to a conversion of the soul that gives us hope that change is possible. And it provides the ability to ask crucial moral questions that can reinvigorate the political discussion.

It's happened before. In both England and the United States, evangelical faith was the catalyst for successful social movements to abolish slavery, end child labour, and secure women's right to vote. More recently, black churches in America, led by Dr Martin Luther King, put their faith into action in the civil rights movement.

Today, we need people who live as if an alternative vision is possible. Especially when real change seems difficult, history needs people who believe that it will happen, and are willing to stake their lives on it. That takes faith. In our time, as in the past, faith can bring people together, motivate and inspire them with a feeling of purpose, an assurance of meaning, and a sense of direction.

This latest volume in Steve Chalke's *Faithworks* series addresses these questions forthrightly. He examines how and why Christian faith became privatized, what we can do about it in the twenty-first century, and offers practical suggestions for the reader on how to get involved in a church that serves its community.

Steve believes, as I do, that a true faith must be put into practice. Action preserves a genuine faith, while an authentic faith maintains the integrity of our actions. The apostle James wrote, 'Faith without works is dead.' Steve is bringing together these vital ingredients for a powerful movement – faith and action. And he understands that history is best changed by social movements which have a spiritual foundation. The Faithworks Campaign is that kind of movement.

Jim Wallis

1. Turning the Tide:
Faithworks Spirituality

I've a definite sense of spirituality. I want Brooklyn to be christened, but I don't know into what religion yet.
David Beckham

Everyone is talking about spirituality; it's the twenty-first-century buzz-word. From the big screen to conversations in local coffee shops, spirituality is a word that is in vogue. Type 'spirituality' into an Internet search engine and you'll find yourself bombarded with no fewer than three million possible websites to sample. One of the obvious reasons for this popularity is that a multi-ethnic, multi-religious, multi-everything society permits a certain ambiguity or vagueness. Its 'looseness' is a huge bonus when the rage of the age is pluralism, promoting tolerance as the virtue to outstrip all others. 'Spirituality' is truly a transreligious word. From the organized religious traditions to Paganism, Jainism or even the highly fashionable eclectic and often exotic 'cut-and-paste' DIY variations – all are claimed to be equally valid spiritualities.

With the triumph of image over substance, spirituality is now also marked by superficiality. It has become the domain of the cool and trendy – a niche in popular culture to be inhabited by those who want to appear 'progressive'. If the nineties were 'green' and hallmarked by an emphasis on environmental issues, then the 'noughties' are blue and nebulously spiritual. But the result of all this 'blue-sky' thinking is that the actual content of spirituality is now almost immaterial. Spirituality has become an end in itself rather than a means to an end. It doesn't matter what you believe, so long as you believe something. Packaging has become far more important than content. In our image- and label-conscious society, style reigns over essence.

> *Suddenly, it's trendy to be spiritual . . . what was once regarded as a minority interest – the preserve of idealists who patronized wholefood shops, burned joss-sticks and read the works of eastern mystics – has now become big business.*
> John Drane

Me, myself and I!

Not so long ago, a friend of mine overheard a conversation between two twenty-something women in a London book-shop. 'I'm just not convinced I want to buy into Zen Buddhism totally,' one said to the other, 'but it does seem to make sense of the struggle and discontentment I'm experiencing in life at the moment . . . and it does have kudos!'

One of the greatest sociological phenomena that has affected spirituality is *consumerism*. Consumerism is about choices, and it teaches us to make them in such a way that we always understand ourselves to be the primary beneficiary. So, the smart choice is always the one that involves minimum input or investment to gain maximum output; 'value-added' is the name of the game.

As one of your lifestyle choices, you might choose a spirituality. This choice is likely to be based on your own particular biases or desires, in much the same way as you might choose whether or not to join a specific gym or fitness centre, or to wear certain clothing labels over and against any others. Making choices in such a way in our consumerist culture generally means that when it comes to choosing a spirituality, the chances are high that the net benefits are going to favour one person and one person only – you!

The goal of any consumer choice is to supplement satisfaction and meaning or add 'kudos' to life. This, coupled with the understanding that it is *our* 'right' to have *our* needs met, means that even spirituality becomes characterized by *getting* over and against *giving*. So, for example, as one British tabloid recently claimed, 'Madonna, who has been searching for the right spiritual environment in which to raise her daughter Lourdes, has turned to the kabbala. Rabbi Eliyhu Jian is advising the *Evita* star on the philosophy, which includes adherence to a low-fat, non-meat diet and a belief in reincarnation.'

Many approach their spiritual journey as . . . a religious
version of the song 'Mambo Number Five' – a little bit of
gospel language here, a little bit of Celtic wisdom there, a little
bit of karma in the sun.
Edith M. Humphrey

If we are honest, we are all looking for some personal benefit from our faith. However, when that becomes our sole motivation, and personal benefit is seen as the only or central gain of spirituality, we have become narcissistic. In the ancient Greek story, Narcissus caught a glimpse of his reflection in a lake, fell in love with his own image and became utterly self-absorbed. In the same way, postmodern spirituality easily falls into the trap of becoming thoroughly self-centred, forgetting that there is a world in need of transformation.

However, there are also many who have little or no time for such inner convictions and belief structures. For them, public service or activism is the only road worthy of being trodden. They ask, 'Who needs contemplatives when there is so much work to be done?' Their soapbox is the one first constructed by Karl Marx: 'Religion is the opiate of the masses.' Religion, they claim, anaesthetizes people and takes them inside themselves; the struggles they face are all internalized and, as a result, nothing ever gets done. As Marx often claimed, 'The world is changed by revolution not by contemplation.'

Something old, not new!

The church isn't immune to this diversity of opinion. For instance, who can deny that for much of the twentieth century, in both the United States and the UK, there was a tendency on the part of many churches to deal with increasing secularization by retreat? Ghetto life was seen as the best form of defence against 'ungodly' culture, complete with sporadic, evangelistic sorties out into a godless society to bring the lost into the fold. Others could address the task of social development, for they had souls to save. Tragically, this retreat from contamination also proved to be a long march into irrelevancy. I know of one Bible college in Texas which even went as far as advertising its campus as '50 miles from the nearest sin' – presumably to sell its remote location to pious parents worried about their 'precious young darling's' moral safety on leaving home.

Liberal religion has lost its spiritual center. It has become both reactive to conservative religion and captive to the shifting winds of the secular culture. Liberal activism has often lacked any real dynamic of personal conversion and, therefore, transformative power. With liberal religion, social action in the world can become severed from its roots in faith, producing a language and practice that seem more bureaucratic and ideological than spiritual.

Jim Wallis

Meanwhile, other sections of Christendom, unimpressed with this negative, head-in-the-sand, 'holy-huddle' mentality, reacted to it and the pressure of their surrounding culture by throwing themselves with all their energy and commitment into politics and social engagement. Rather than saving souls, their eyes became firmly set on shaping society. But unfortunately, as we all know, in the desperate search to 'fit' the prevailing secular culture, many slowly lost any semblance of Christian distinctiveness or genuine spirituality.

Two sides of the same coin

In truth, to subscribe to either the 'otherworldly' notion of Christian spirituality, which is all about the inner life, or alternatively to opt for the 'activist' public service option, is to entirely abandon truly biblically rooted Christian spirituality. Biblically, no separation exists between the inner and outer life; they are two sides of the same coin. To talk about inner versus outer life, religion versus politics, or intercessors versus activists, is to attempt to drive a wedge between that which by nature is unified, thus producing a perilous and destructive dualism which can only survive by turning its back on the teaching of both the Old and New Testaments.

Spirituality that is focused on the inner life is dead, and for the most part falls foul of the criticisms which Freud and others have made of religion – that it is no more than a crutch for the weak. Likewise, mission, activism and public service that becomes detached from an inner spirituality will ultimately prove bankrupt of transformational power and energy.

> *The word integrity indicates 'wholeness' and to achieve it requires a harmony between the public and private life. That which we claim to be aware of in our souls must become visible before it is credible. Likewise, our actions need to spring from the depths of our spirit if they are to be of substance and significance.*
> Mike Riddell

History shows us that when this separation or dualism is present, it is all too easy to become either isolated from culture (which we could call the *sacralization* of our faith) or seduced by culture, leading to the secularization of our faith. Either way, faith becomes impotent and sterile; genuine Christian spirituality is lost, and the light that should be shining in the darkness is extinguished.

Rediscovery not reinvention

The Bible will not allow for either of these mistakes to be made. It contradicts the sacred/secular divide and calls for faith and activity to function in harmony with one another. In fact, it does not recognize any distinction between the two – the Old Testament word for 'faith' also implies 'faithfulness', i.e. obedient activity.

Our faith is the source of our action: it is our engine; our inspiration; our reason; our motivation. Yet at the same time our involvement in society informs, deepens, sharpens and authenticates that faith. Or, to put it as bluntly as the New Testament does, faith without works is dead (James 2:17). Authentic Christian faith requires us to be with God for other people, and with other people for God.

Jesus himself provides us with the foundational statement for Christian orthodoxy that makes everything else in the Bible look like a commentary on it: 'Love the Lord your God with all your heart and with all your soul and with all your mind . . . Love your neighbour as yourself' (Matthew 22:37–39); the two are inextricably connected. The ability to love your neighbour as yourself is funded by loving God. Your love for God is authenticated by loving your neighbour.

Love must work to be real! Love acts, and only in so doing demonstrates its worth and authenticity. That is why Paul tells us that while we were still in the mess we were in, God loved us and sent his Son for us (Romans 5:8). What good would a God be who, having declared that he *is* love, left us to stew in our messy, fallen world? Such love would echo hollow, worthless and fake. In the same way, 1 John 4:8 reminds us, 'Whoever does not love does not know God, because God is love.' So, as St Francis of Assisi reminds us, we are to work to sow love where there is hatred, pardon where there is injury, faith where there is doubt, hope where there is despair, light where there is darkness, and joy where there is sadness. This is the nuts and bolts, the stuff and matter of biblical spirituality – this is faith that works!

> *When St Paul said, 'Come out and be separate,' he did not mean that Christians ought to take no interest in anything on earth except religion. To neglect science, art, literature and politics – to read nothing which is not directly spiritual – to know nothing about what is going on among mankind, and never to look at a newspaper – to care nothing about the government of one's own country, and to be utterly indifferent to the persons who guide its counsels and make its laws – all this may seem very right and proper in the eyes of some people. But I take leave to think that it is an idle, selfish neglect of duty.*
>
> J. C. Ryle

Point proven?

'There are three things I don't like about you.' The then head of the Council Housing Department wasn't a man to mince his words. I'd just outlined our plan to set up a small, referred-access hostel for homeless young people in his borough, and he was somewhat underwhelmed by our proposal, to say the least.

'First,' he explained, sneering at me as I sat in his office, 'you're a Christian. Second, you're an *evangelical* Christian.' After these two, I wondered what would come next. 'Third,' he announced, 'you're a *minister*. We don't need any hostels run by your type around here. If you open, it'll be over my dead body!'

I don't know what happened to him, but we *did* open. It took over four years to turn our vision into a reality, but we managed it. What's more, Oasis, the charity I started 18 years ago with the specific aim of opening that one hostel, now runs a wide range of different facilities for homeless and vulnerable people in London's inner city.

And our approach works: figures from that first hostel show that around 80 per cent of the young people who've stayed there and then been 'resettled' by us have held down a job and stayed in housing for at least three years after leaving. They're making a contribution to the community around them rather than remaining the 'victims' of society.

In spite of the vehement protests of their Head of Housing almost two decades ago, that local council is now in absolutely no doubt just how good a job we do. A senior representative of that same London borough council admitted to me recently that our resettlement figures were impressive – in fact, they were ones he wished other hostels on his patch could emulate.

Faith works! Genuine Christian faith brings transformation – both inner and outer. If you asked any of our staff why they were prepared to work long hours for comparatively little pay, or why their job gave them such enjoyment, or why they don't give up on our clients or residents, their faith would come at the very top of their list of reasons.

*Many people mistake our work for our vocation. Our vocation
is the love of Jesus.*
Mother Teresa

The church and Faithworks

Christianity was, at its birth, a transforming movement of
the Holy Spirit. The accounts in the book of Acts tell us
about a God who was, and is, engaged with his world.
From creation, through to the incarnation and the birth of
the church, God is intimately involved. And, committed to
this principle, the Christian church must also be engaged
and involved.

It is no accident that we have been left a legacy by the
Old Testament prophets whose task it was constantly to
underline the fact that God is interested in every dimen-
sion of people's lives. It is no accident that Jesus himself
did not simply present the world with a set of propositions
to be believed, but came to demonstrate that God is passionately concerned with the needs of communities and
individuals at every level.

Intimacy with God and involvement with society are
inseparably connected. Jesus' final words to his disciples,
as recorded by Matthew, are: 'Go . . . And surely I am with
you always' (Matthew 28:19–20). So it is that the 'stay-at-
home' church can never know the intimacy it so craves, for
it is in the act of 'going' that we encounter the risen Jesus.
True intimacy with God is the outcome of our involvement
in his world. Involvement in God's world is the outcome

of genuine intimacy. Intimacy and involvement belong together – to ignore one is always to destroy the quality and depth of the other.

Jesus' self-declared intent was to usher in the kingdom of God, which was about nothing less than wholeness and well-being or, to use the Old Testament term, *shalom*. And with the words 'Go and make disciples of all nations . . .', he commissioned us to extend the borders of the kingdom into the present world – indwelt, energized, guided and directed by the Spirit of God.

The greatest poverty our nation and world face is a poverty of hope. This is why the Christian faith is potent, the Christian message is vital and the community of the church has such a unique role to play in society. Genuine Christian faith brings hope that transforms lives. Authentic Christian spirituality works!

The Faithworks Movement is therefore committed to three goals:

1. To empower and inspire every local church to redis-cover its role at the hub of the community.
2. To challenge and change the public perception of the church by engaging with both media and government.
3. To promote Christian values within our society.

Government is increasingly realizing that one of the keys to unlocking the problems on our streets and in our communities is faith-motivated initiatives. The church, which was the original welfare-provider, still has an indispens-able role to play as we enter the twenty-first century. It is the purpose of this book, and indeed of the Faithworks Movement, to inspire the church to fulfil that role once again, through the rediscovery of genuine Christian spirituality, the hallmarks of which are always intimacy and involvement.

> *Christianity is more than a matter of a new understanding*
> *... right living is more a challenge than right thinking. The*
> *challenge is not the intellectual one but the political one – the*
> *creation of a new people who have aligned themselves with the*
> *seismic shift that has occurred in the world since Christ.*
> Stanley Hauerwas

Going further

1. What are the things that distinguish authentic Christianity from popular superficial spirituality?
2. In the Western world where the consumer is king, how can we begin to restore selfless Christianity?
3. Jesus calls us to be in the world, but not of it; most of us are of the world but not in it! How can we be relevant without being compromised?
4. Read Matthew 25:31–46. In this teaching of Jesus, why does he place such significance on doing good works? Does this passage worry you at all? How can we allow the teaching of Jesus to affect our daily lives?

2. Intimacy and Involvement: *Spirituality in the Old Testament*

'The art of great acting is learning to immerse yourself totally in the world of your script,' explained the drama student. 'It's one of the most difficult yet essential elements of theatre. But it's the only way you can ever really learn to embody your character on stage.' Reflecting on her comments, I thought that her insight reflected exactly the church's task when it comes to grappling with the Bible. It too requires us to immerse or re-imagine ourselves in the drama of the ancient Israelites and their journey with God. It challenges us to re-inhabit their world and see through their eyes in order to understand more accurately the context and content of its pages.

> *The Old Testament is absorbed with what it means to be the living people of the living God.*
> Chris Wright

Just like George Lucas's now instantly recognizable opening to the *Star Wars* films, with the rolling script disappearing into the distance, we could read the words, 'A long time ago, in a land far, far away, the Lord said to Abram . . .' (Genesis 12), as the beginning of the epic from which the greatest movement the world has ever seen would grow.

'Much that once was, is lost, for none live who could remember it. Some things that should not have been forgotten were lost. History became legend. Legend became myth.' Tragically, these words, written by J. R. R. Tolkien about the mysterious ring in his famous book, *The Fellowship of the Ring*, could equally be true of modern-day Christianity. The church has forgotten to remember its roots, and in forgetting to remember, much has been lost.

> *History is bunk.*
> Henry Ford

Czeslaw Milosz, winner of the 1980 Nobel Prize for Literature, remarked in his acceptance speech in Stockholm that our age is characterized by a 'refusal to remember'. Unfortunately, the church is not immune to the problems of its surrounding culture. Seduced by the moment, it has lost its memory and as a consequence found itself orphaned from its past, spiritually vulnerable and ill-equipped for the challenges that confront it.

Rather than understanding our faith in the context of its ancient Judaeo-Christian foundations, we often behave as though it simply fell out of the sky yesterday as a pre-packaged, 'ready-to-go' twenty-first-century Western religion.

One result of this 'disconnection' is that the Old Testament is rarely read in its fullness or richness. This has had deeply unfortunate consequences because the New Testament is written in such a way as to presuppose the content of the Old Testament. Its writers presumed that anyone reading their stories or letters would already be at least vaguely familiar with what was written before. So, for instance, when Peter speaks of (or Paul writes about) the coming of the Messiah, he would have understood Jesus and his task within the framework of the Jewish thought he inherited and assumed that his hearers also made this vital connection.

Jews don't 'read' the Bible. We sing it, argue with it, wrestle with it, listen to it and turn it inside out to find a new insight we had missed before.
Jonathan Sacks

Rootless

In so far as the church in the West has forgotten its roots, we have left ourselves impoverished and have neglected, even abandoned, authentic Christian spirituality. That is why so many Christians find themselves bereft of anything but the most superficial clues as to how to articulate their faith in a way that is integrated with the rest of life. Faith has been reduced to nothing more than a 'bolt-on accessory' which regrettably has little impact on overall lifestyle. As a result, countless Christians either learn to live with a constant nagging guilt or grow hard and cynical learning not to think about such 'deep' issues. Life, for most people, is neatly compartmentalized into religion, social life, work, leisure and so on – faith is down as a 'Sunday thing'.

> *We need to come through our disorientation to a reorientation, a return to our biblical roots, that propels us forward to grapple with life in a postmodern culture. [We need] a renewed encounter with the historic Christian faith that takes seriously where we have come historically. It is only this sort of reorientation that will be able to provide us with genuine hope and critical guidance as we move into the twenty-first century.*
>
> J. Richard Middleton and Brian J. Walsh

Conversely, we all know of those over-enthusiastic Christians who aren't satisfied unless everything is 'spiritual'. Not only is their language littered and punctuated with endless religious clichés, but every incidental happening in life is interpreted through spiritually tinted spectacles and loaded with higher meaning. Even the mundane is quickly transformed into the miraculous while those who cannot see are dismissed as 'lacking in insight'.

But though this kind of faith seems all-consuming, in truth it is impotent. Its hallmark is not depth but superficiality. It is born not of intimacy but of naïveté. Whether its root is escapism or melodrama, it is neither helpful nor biblical and, more often than not, it's also extremely embarrassing.

So what does a genuine, biblically informed and rooted spirituality look like? To answer this it is necessary to engage in that act which is vital to the survival of any community – *remembering*.

Spirituality the Hebrew way: creation and caretaking

'The earth is the Lord's,' declares Psalm 24:1, to which Psalm 115:16 adds, 'He has given [it] to man.' In other words, there is an inseparable connection between us and creation – a connection which is hard to fathom because we sophisticated Westerners have lost touch with it. We are separated from it by leather soles, rubber tyres, glass, metal and a host of other synthetic products. But the Bible reminds us of our intimate link with creation. God, in his generosity, has placed us on this beautiful planet and given us the responsibility to be its caretakers (Genesis 1:26ff). We are its trustees or stewards. It's not every day you find appointments like that in the local jobcentre!

One of the ways we can try and grapple with how to fulfil this vocation is to look at God's relationship with the nation of Israel. For instance, the laws, statutes and ordinances given to the people, by God, throughout the book of Leviticus were wide-ranging. From healthy eating to family affairs; from medical advice to farming instructions; from correct religious protocol to international relations – most areas of community and national life had some light shed on them by the Hebrew Scriptures.

But if you could travel back in a time capsule and ask the Israelites how they found time for their spiritual life with all of this creation-tending legislation to contend with, they would look at you a little confused. This *was* spiritual! Worship was an attitude or approach to the whole of life. There was no divorce or separation between the seemingly mundane and the more formal religious practices in the Old Testament. Administration and legislation were part of worship. Tending the soil, caring for the animals, harvesting the crops and sustaining the relationships of the community were acts of thankfulness and worship to God. And since every aspect of living in the land of Israel was bound up with living in relationship with God, it was natural for the Hebrew Scriptures to contain political (politics simply means 'the affairs of the people') and social laws relating to the warp and weft of daily life.

It's easy to see the reason that some people, without understanding this context, wonder why we have book after book in the Old Testament devoted to what appear to be tedious laws and boring bureaucracy. But the truth is, the Scriptures weren't written with the intention of being either a 'Sunday book' or a devotional manual to provide inspiration in those 'special' moments. The writer of Deuteronomy comments: 'Impress them [God's laws] on your children. Talk about them when you sit at home and when you walk along the road, when you lie down and when you get up. Tie them as symbols on your hands and bind them on your foreheads. Write them on the doorframes of your houses and on your gates' (Deuteronomy 6:7–9). Israelites were thoroughly convinced that their sacred writings instructed every aspect of life that was lived in its totality before God. Authentic Hebrew spirituality was about 'joined-up' living.

> There is nothing more pathetic in religious life than witnessing the noisy and frenzied rattling of spiritual sabers that have long ceased to carry a cutting edge. The only spiritual reality we are called to . . . is down on earth. As Metropolitan Anthony once put it, we need 'a spiritual reality that operates at the level of the kitchen sink'.
>
> Andrew Walker

In fact, on many occasions when the children of Israel got over-focused on what many in our culture would more narrowly define as the religious or spiritual dimensions of life, God spoke through his prophets, criticizing them for their preoccupation with fasting and praying, calling instead for mercy and justice in public life. See for example Isaiah 1:10–20; 58. It was not that the fasting and praying were inherently bad, but issues of injustice and oppression went by the board because the people mistakenly thought they were embarking on the more noble enterprise of being spiritual. God soon put them straight, letting them know that the blessings they sought were only going to be provided if they put their house in order and sorted out what we would (misguidedly) understand as the more mundane issues of life.

The Bible is clear: the living out of Israel's covenant obligations could not be restricted to the narrowly 'spiritual'. To focus on the religious at the expense of the civic arenas of life was to abandon true spirituality. Everything was to be considered as being in relation to God. Biblical spirituality was an integrated spirituality. Outward engagement was as essential as inner orientation. Authentic spirituality was about intimacy and involvement. Both were essential if the nation of Israel was to fulfil its role – representing God to creation.

Human identity and community

God is community – Father, Son and Spirit. Thus, God, by definition, relates. And God made us in his image – so we too are relational beings. This is why the doctrine of the Trinity is of such great and practical importance, especially in a society plagued by loneliness and the problems of isolation.

Human identity is found in relating. Unlike the French philosopher Descartes, who tried to reduce existence to the rational process of thinking, famously declaring: 'I think therefore I am,' the Bible instructs us that true existence lies within the context of relationship – 'I am known, therefore I am'.

This quest for relationship is seen clearly in the film

Castaway. The main character, played by Tom Hanks, stranded following a plane crash on a deserted and exotic equatorial paradise-island, is so starved of company that he draws a face on a volleyball, gives it the name 'Wilson' and enters into a conversation (albeit one-sided) with it! As individuals, we are incomplete. We are not made to be alone. We crave relationship. Only here can we find fulfilment as humans and understand what it really means to be a person. Only in this context do we find the answer to the question the human race has asked since the dawn of creation – who am I?

> *It is communion which makes beings 'be' – nothing exists without it, not even God.*
> John Zizioulas

In the story of Genesis 2, Adam (the first man God creates), just like Tom Hanks' character in *Castaway*, was incomplete. So God provided someone for him. Importantly, it was someone who was different – Eve. Difference or otherness is an essential ingredient to relationship. Just as the three persons of the Trinity are different, so is each human being. In fact, it is at this fundamental point that the biblical doctrine of the Trinity and its understanding of community differs from that of Communism. Communism attempted to build community on the basis that everyone should be the same in order to belong – and failed! It failed because it is part of our DNA that we are each unique and special. This truth makes uniformity a possibility in theory but renders it an impossibility in reality. In stark contrast to all this, the biblical understanding of community, relationship and belonging maintains diversity, while at the same time emphasizing unity and togetherness. This means that we can all be part of the whole without in any way feeling threatened or insecure because someone is different from us. Completeness is found in the sum of the unique parts, each of which is made to be part of the whole.

The core building block of community in the Old Testament is the family. However, Hebrew family (unlike today's concept of nuclear family) was sprawling and composed of several generations. Within this context, each individual involved could find the support, love and affirmation they needed in order to thrive. Each family then plugged into the wider community (or tribe) and, in turn, the community into the nation. Everyone had a place and there was a place for everyone. We might call it a 'living human web'.

Within this web, identity was formed and needs were met. Or at least they should have been. Again, the infectious relational disease the Bible calls sin tended to disrupt or threaten the fabric of these horizontal relationships just as much as the vertical one with God. So it is that, for example, Jeremiah thunders: 'Do not oppress the alien, the fatherless or the widow' (Jeremiah 7:6). Here were three categories of people who could find themselves outside of the arms of the inclusive Hebrew family and thus of the community, which is why God shouts to his people, 'Get them in, and get them in now!'

Community breakdown

Westerners today do not think the way the ancient Hebrews did. If the Jews were a people marked by thinking corporately and living collectively, our contemporary culture is marked by a sense of individualism and self-fulfilment. This has had a massive impact and as a result, by and large, family and community life have become a distant national memory.

It was John Donne, the seventeenth-century writer and Dean of St Paul's Cathedral, who famously declared that 'no man is an island'. In his recent book, *About a Boy*, Nick Hornby explores this concept from a twenty-first-century perspective. The tragedy is, he claims, that today it is widely believed that 'every man is an island'. Our society has become fragmented. It bears the wounds of deep-rooted individualism. But there is also a great longing to belong, to be welcomed and valued, not for what we do, but just for who we are. This loneliness or exclusion, coupled with the drive for significance, is one of the most recognizable symptoms of our age.

Loneliness is one of the most universal sources of human suffering today . . . Children, adolescents, adults, and old people are in growing degree exposed to the contagious disease of loneliness in a world in which a competitive individualism tries to reconcile itself with a culture that speaks about togetherness . . .

Henri Nouwen

Anthony Giddens, Director of the London School of Economics, has conducted one of the most comprehensive surveys of relationship trends in the Western world to date. His conclusions focus on a type of relationship that is characterized by what he terms 'flotation'. His argument is that relationships nowadays exist on the surface, without depth and without any permanence. Social relations are entered into for their own sake, 'for what can be derived' or gained, only to be dropped once either of the parties believes their individual satisfaction is at an end.

Similarly, Harvard professor Robert Putnam catalogues the breakdown in community and society in his book *Bowling Alone*. He claims that healthy societies are built on a vast network of socially and economically beneficial, formal and informal relationships. As these relationships are allowed to deteriorate and people grow isolated, rates of crime, depression and suicide rise. But it's not only people at the bottom end of the social spectrum who feel the pain – corporate bosses and executive employees are equally susceptible. As a result, materially speaking, standards of living may never have been higher, but happiness and fulfilment are at a very low ebb. Another consequence is that with isolation comes a loss of identity. Personality becomes stunted, enfeebled, and in general people emotionally, mentally and spiritually fade away. For example, when Diana, Princess of Wales, in the now-famous BBC television interview, told her interrogator, Martin Bashir, of the conspiracy to isolate her, she observed, 'And the best way to dismantle a personality is to isolate it.'

Not too long ago, I recall reading about the Duke of

Westminster in an article in *The Times*. Discussing his
wife's ongoing battle with breast cancer, he lamented
the fact that, despite his estimated £2.1 billion fortune, he
was deeply unhappy and required a daily diet of anti-
depressants. It was not until he resolved to 'clear his diary
and spend more time with his wife of 20 years and their
four children' that any kind of release began to come.
Within this simple illustration lies part of the antidote to
today's despondency: relationship and belonging.

> *Human community expresses a profound, elemental desire for*
> *. . . contact with other human souls, just as in the flesh there*
> *is the urge for physical merger with other flesh.*
> Dietrich Bonhoeffer

The Jewish antidote

A non-Jewish friend of mine who lives in a predominantly
liberal Jewish community in north London has always
been amazed at the depth of solidarity he has found
among them. Frequently, he's been asked to come and participate in their Sabbath meals, despite the fact that he
doesn't share the same faith commitments. But this inclusivity isn't for the purpose of making him one of their own;
it's simply their desire to include and form relationships.

Relationships for ancient and contemporary Jews were
and are intimately linked to worship. How you interacted
with others was a big part of belonging to God. This is one

of the reasons the Ten Commandments (Exodus 20) take the shape they do; they are all to do with relationships. The first four are about our vertical relationship with God and the remaining six, which grow out from them, are about our horizontal relationships with others. The Bible's teaching is unequivocal: we find our human identity in the way we interact and engage with God and others. It's about inclusivity and community.

The individualism which has affected our society has also affected our Christianity. Our tendency today is to try to shrink our spirituality to simply a vertical relationship with God. So we speak of 'my personal Saviour' or 'my walk with God' and read books or go to seminars that are entitled 'Knowing God's call on my life'. But this 'bowling alone' spirituality is alien to the Bible. Such exclusivity is self-absorbingly ugly. Craig Gay comments: 'As the discovery and formation of individual identity has become a predominantly private activity, it seems we have been cut loose from the discipline of community.'

When we look at one another, we see not only a face that is being looked at by God, we see a person from whom God cannot bear to be parted; so how can we bear it? Any divisions in our world, class, race, church loyalty, have to be confronted with the painful truth that apparently we find it easier than God does to manage without certain bits of the human creation.

Rowan Williams

True human identity is forged on two equally important planes: one is our intimacy or relationship with God, the other is our belonging to and involvement in community. Intimacy and involvement: it is here that we locate self-worth, identity, fulfilment and the 'how to' of creation stewardship.

I love, therefore I am.
Kallistos Ware

Foundations for Christian spirituality

Around the world each Friday evening, today just as through the centuries, Jewish families celebrate the beginning of the Sabbath with a meal together. But if you were to pose the question of when exactly they do the worship bit of it all – before, during or after the meal? – they would look at you askance. Their rejoinder might well be something along the lines of, 'Don't you Gentiles know any better than that? The whole occasion is worship. From the reading of the Torah to the praying; from the eating of the food to the drinking of wine; from the laughter to the story telling; from embracing each other to singing together. It is *all* worship.'

The Sabbath meal is Old Testament spirituality in a nutshell. Compressed into this simple event is the whole gamut of life and holistic spirituality: the enjoyment of God, the enjoyment of each other and the enjoyment of creation. This is the bedrock upon which is built true authentic Christian spirituality.

Going further

1. Given that 'remembering' is so important to a healthy spirituality, how can we help ourselves in this area?
2. In the light of the biblical mandate to take care of God's creation, how seriously, and in what ways, should we be getting involved in 'green issues'?
3. Name three or four groups/clubs/societies that you belong to (including church). What, if anything, is different about being a part of church?
4. What, if any, are the ways your church is making a positive impact on your local community? What other things could you do to encourage community building rather than community breakdown?
5. Spiritualities condoning withdrawal and isolation are not always helpful. How can our faith communities (be they rural or urban) avoid this peril?
6. In what ways would contemporary Christian spirituality be richer if we remembered our roots in Old Testament spirituality?

3. Intimacy and Involvement: *Spirituality in the New Testament*

Some think Jesus was essentially a teacher with a gift for delivering the most stirring of monologues. Others have credited him as a master philosopher because of the depth and profundity of his teaching. Still others have regarded him as the great moralist and labelled him a brilliant preacher. But as popular as each of these descriptions is, none of them entirely squares with the facts. Jesus was not a typical teacher, philosopher or preacher because he didn't just deliver eloquent speeches or think nebulous and grandiose thoughts. First and foremost he did things, and then, where necessary, offered comment.

Teachers instruct but often in speech and theory only. Philosophers observe, think and write but are usually detached from the reality which most other people inhabit. Preachers can easily fall into the trap of proclaiming lofty ideals that should more often than not have the caveat: 'Do as I say, not as I do.' Jesus was never guilty of any of these charges. His teaching was bound up in his actions, which were always authenticating his words. This in turn meant he was able to commend people not just to do as he said, but to do as he did! And unlike philosophers, his thinking was never abstract or removed – it was always informed and engaged. It's for these reasons that many of his contemporaries began to regard him as a prophet.

The Jewish prophets offered a whole new vantage point from which to see the world. They were spokesmen whose risky vocation was to provide a counter-agenda to the often corrupt and deficient political systems of the day. They, under God's authority and in relationship with him, stood against the status quo, critiquing existing structures in society and pointing it in new directions. The form of this critique included high-profile actions pregnant with symbolic meaning as well as a resolute outspokenness. It's vital to note, however, that this involvement in society stemmed directly from a deep intimacy with God. For instance, it was only after the prophet Isaiah encountered God powerfully in the Temple that he engaged in the risky adventure of pointing Judah to a different vision and approach to national life (Isaiah 6).

A prophet holds the Bible in one hand and the newspaper in the other – reads both and allows one to inform his understanding of the other.
Charles Spurgeon

Jesus was a prophet. Through him, God was staging a challenge to the world and ushering in a counter-agenda to those already existing in Israel. Through a combination of highly symbolic actions, such as upturning traders' tables in the Temple or eating with the 'wrong' people, as well as by reinterpreting the Old Testament Scriptures in his teaching, Jesus was engaging in nothing less than a highly political and risky revolution – a revolution known as the kingdom of God.

> *A prophet is a human person who is admitted to Yahweh's cabinet and thus becomes another means of executing heaven's decisions on earth and a transmitter of messages between earth and heaven. This works both ways, for the prophet intercedes in the cabinet, speaking on earth's behalf there, as well as bringing announcements of heaven's decisions.*
> John Goldingay

A new deal?

Herod the Great's reign was balanced on a knife-edge. Palestine was as volatile then as it is today. Each day was lived out under the constant threat of coups and revolutions. Aware of the fragility of his rule, Herod was constantly sensitive to any possible threat of over-throw. Even the stirrings of an infant in a stable in Bethlehem could potentially destabilize his governance and therefore needed nipping in the bud.

But, if Herod needed to take note of this seemingly innocuous event in Bethlehem, the Roman Empire needed to more so. Herod was powerful, but his power paled before the might of Caesar Augustus. As the grand-nephew and adopted son of Julius Caesar, it was he who turned what had become a rocky republic into the greatest and most famous empire of them all. As the establisher and sole leader of the Roman Empire (27 BC to AD 14), he had his own 'gospel' for the people of Israel, the 'good news' according to Caesar: 'Divine Augustus Caesar, son of god, imperator of land and sea, the benefactor and saviour of the whole world, has brought you peace.' Anyone else laying claim to this title would have been treated as a blasphemer and permanently silenced. Therefore, when the God of Israel sent his messenger, Gabriel, to announce that the true Saviour of the world and bringer of real peace, the *shalom* of God, was now present on earth (Luke 2:11, 14), it was political dynamite. Jesus was the new kid on the block, a pretender to the throne. The gauntlet had been thrown down.

One of the fundamental reasons that Augustus' gospel needed challenging was because it was exclusive and narrow. The benefits and peace that Augustus claimed to bring were only ever enjoyed by the élite and privileged. In contrast, those who spent their lives on the margins of society heard Caesar's rhetoric but experienced none of the promises. In reality, Augustus' gospel only served to create a bigger chasm between the haves and the have-nots. It fed a system of corruption and injustice in which the people without a voice always lost. What was really needed was a new 'gospel', a new deal, a deal which was comprehensive and accessible to all, notwithstanding social status, gender or heritage.

Jesus and his messianic mandate

*Christian ascetism called the world evil and abandoned it.
Humanity is waiting for a Christian revolution which will
call the world evil and change it.*
Walter Rauschenbusch

Expectation makes for an exciting plot. One film which
thrives on it is the Wachowski brothers' blockbuster *The
Matrix*. In the movie, 'the Oracle' predicts the coming of
'the One' who will bring an end to the artificially generated world simulated by machines. These machines,
created by artificial intelligence, harvest their energy from
an imprisoned and anaesthetized human race. But the sus-
pense and excitement of the film turns on the question of
whether or not Neo (an anagram of 'one') is the long-
expected chosen one who would bring release and
freedom from this unreality and slavery by realizing the
truth. The Matrix has a remarkable parallel with the
accounts the New Testament writers give us of Jesus and
what came to be known as the messianic expectation.

The Jewish Scriptures predicted a Messiah who would
be anointed by God, and through him an end to the
oppression that the Jews had so long experienced under
successive Roman occupations. In fact, so intense was the
longing for this deliverer, that self-professed messiahs
were a dime a dozen, though up until that point, none had
come up with the goods. Then, on an eventful day in his
home town of Nazareth, Jesus, who was by now gaining

some public recognition, entered the local synagogue. He picked up a scroll and read a passage from the text of the prophet Isaiah (Luke 4:18–30), which all present would have understood as a direct reference to the coming of the promised Messiah, poignantly adding: 'Today this scripture is fulfilled in your hearing.' Initially, his words were greeted by his hearers with astonishment. God's long-awaited favour was about to be poured out upon them. But as he continued, their attitude began to change. In referring to the activities of Elijah, who brought God's grace to a widowed woman who was not a Jew, and Elisha, who did the same for a Syrian whose leprosy even further reinforced his alien status and therefore banishment from the community of God's people (Leviticus 14), Jesus was making a significant statement. The implication was clear: God's salvation or *shalom* was no longer to be mainly restricted to Israel – it was for everyone. Those normally considered beyond the pale were now invited to be part of God's people. God's kingdom was now transnational and all-inclusive, regardless of race, colour, gender, creed or social class – from now on, all people were God's people.

At this point, those listening began to get agitated. 'Who does he think he is?' 'What right has he got to turn his back on the established rights of the chosen Jewish nation?' Their agitation soon became outrage. Their initial astonishment at Jesus' words turned to anger and indignation, to the point not only of chasing him out of the synagogue, but also right out of town. So it was that Jesus' original audience demonstrated their complete inability to cope with the reality of

God's outrageous, all-inclusive love – tragically, a trait they
have shared with countless others since.

> *Throughout his brief public career, Jesus spoke and acted as if
> God's plan of salvation and justice for Israel and the world
> was being unveiled through his own presence, his own work,
> his own fate.*
> Tom Wright

It was the New Testament scholar Professor Howard
Marshall who famously commented, 'Over the course of
the last couple of decades I can recollect only two occasions on which I have heard sermons specifically devoted
to the theme of the kingdom of God . . . I find this silence
rather surprising because it is universally agreed by New
Testament scholars that the central theme of the teaching of
Jesus was the kingdom of God.'

The reason every Jewish pulse raced and heart throbbed
when the kingdom was mentioned was because they knew
that it was going to radically alter the way things were –
right there, right then! Socially, politically, economically
and even religiously – the dawn of God's kingdom meant
change. And that's exactly what Jesus was talking about,
only on a far more radical scale than his hearers ever
thought about. He wasn't advocating some other-worldly
'pie in the sky when you die' spirituality. Jesus understood
that through him God was enacting a new order for this
present world. 'An order,' Chrys Caragounis writes, 'in

which humankind could see the fulfilment of its ultimate desires for righteousness, peace, justice, happiness, freedom from sin and guilt, and a restored relationship to God – an order in which God was king.'

The word 'religion' has its roots in the Latin word meaning 'reconnection'. Jesus was bringing *true* religion because, through him, reconnection was being forged at every level – relationships restored interpersonally within humanity, between humanity and creation, and between humanity and God. Salvation is inclusive in the widest sense; not only was it not restricted to Jews – it was not restricted to people. According to John, God's love was so great for the *whole* world that he sent Jesus (John 3:16–17). Far from being individualist and exclusive, what Jesus was doing was not only corporate but cosmic, even universal in its implications. God's goal was to redeem not just Israel but the whole creation from the destructive consequences of sin. That's why today a growing number of biblical scholars have started describing salvation as *re-creation* – the process of remaking creation in the way that it was before humankind's rebellion started wreaking cosmic havoc. Jesus was, in Henri Nouwen's words, 'making all things new'.

A message for everyone

As far as the authorities were concerned, it was 'the usual suspects' who followed Jesus – the people they labelled as 'sinners' or 'the poor' – those condemned to spend life on the margins or periphery of society. However, the term 'poor' wasn't solely a reference to economic poverty or material destitution as we tend to think of it today; it was wider than that. It referred to all those people who, for one reason or another, had fallen into the category of shame that warranted isolation and exclusion from the people of God. One of the most striking aspects of Jesus' speech and actions was that it was these very outcasts who benefited from his mission. Not because it was restricted to them, but simply because most often they were the ones who had the greatest recognition of their need and could spot that what he was offering was different, real and tangible. If all Jesus had been doing was pushing an abstract theological formula or the usual religious/political propaganda, these people would have walked away. Instead, they considered that he was worth listening to. In fact, they concluded that they would be fools to disregard him. His message was fantastic. It was real good news. The best they had ever heard. Real *shalom*, right there, right then – for them.

Occurring more than two hundred and fifty times in the Old Testament, shalom covers well-being in the widest sense of the word, incorporating notions of contentment, health, prosperity, justice, unity and salvation – at individual, communal, national, international and creational levels.
Dr Roger Hurding

Shalom is one of the most profound words in the Bible.

While it is often translated today as 'peace', it has, as Roger Hurding suggests, a much wider meaning than the absence of conflict or the possession of inner tranquillity. In the Old Testament, it refers to comprehensive well-being, or to all round flourishing in every area of life. And this was the concept which both informed and shaped the holistic nature of Jesus' view of salvation. For him, there was no disparity between the physical and spiritual; he was concerned about whole people. But even more than that, rather than simply dealing with individuals, *shalom* was about community well-being. Thus, Jesus was committed to creating a kingdom community, where priorities were different and *shalom* was experienced collectively by all.

By persistently and provocatively choosing to eat, drink and spend his time with those considered beyond the pale ('sinners'), Jesus was inaugurating a new, inclusive community. The company he kept acted as an overt symbol to onlookers that God was intimate with those whom respectable society deemed to be unacceptable. By accepting, befriending and healing the disabled, or, as they were called, 'the unclean', Jesus subverted the Jewish purity laws and showed that he placed a higher premium on relationships than on misplaced etiquettes and laws. But his acts were not only a sign that God was on the side of the humiliated and rejected – they demonstrated that he was taking the initiative and going to them before they made any moves towards him.

In telling parables such as the Prodigal Son (Luke 15:11–32), Jesus turned commonplace expectations upside down and portrayed God running to welcome the weak and the outcast, thereby removing their shame and restoring their honour. In his story of Lazarus and the rich man (Luke 16:19–31), Jesus denounced behaviour like that of the Pharisees. He showed that the new community centred around him will be one that embraces the 'outsider', and those who refuse to acknowledge this will find themselves scandalously moving from a position of perceived 'inside' privilege, to being denied salvation through their own foolishness.

> *Luke portrays Jesus as one who refuses to recognize any social, ethnic, political, or religious barriers. In his boundary-breaking ministry, Jesus embraces all.*
> David Bosch

Jesus: intimate and involved

To truly understand the revolutionary nature of Jesus' response to the social, military and religious oppression of his culture, it's vital to look at the other routes and well-trodden pathways open to those who were dissatisfied with the way things were in first-century Palestine. Refusing to toe Caesar's party line (which was the approach of Herod and the High Priests), the Pharisees were totally committed to the Jewish religious institution. They had little time for compromise with Caesar, but believed that through summoning the nation of Israel to adhere rigorously to Old Testament Law (as interpreted by their own scribes), they would usher in God's kingdom – liberation would only come through piety and strict observance of the Law.

However, there were two other main responses to Roman rule, which, while at opposite ends of the spectrum, shared a common theme: a total inability to cope with alien occupation, and a refusal to compromise with it in any way. The first response meant withdrawing from society altogether to become 'monks'. The best example of this approach were the Essenes (the writers of the Dead Sea Scrolls), who lived in the desert at Qumran on the banks of the River Jordan. They believed that the only viable position open to them was to retreat from the contamination of the world (Roman-run Palestine) and wait in prayer for God to put his master plan of redemption into action. The second response, that of the Zealots, was to pick up arms and prepare to fight a holy and bloody war in which God would deliver victory and show his might over the powers of evil. If the message of the Essenes was 'Retreat, pray and wait for God to act!' that of the Zealots was 'Get stuck in – God helps those who help themselves!'

Against this backdrop, we see just how radical Jesus was. He didn't just recycle the legalistic religiosity of the Pharisees, the passive pathway of the Essenes or the route of Zealot-style terrorism. Instead, his was a genuinely revolutionary approach, one for everyone: the haves and the have-nots, the religious and non-religious, the insiders and outsiders, all bar none.

Jesus' alternative was built on the twin principles of

relationship with God and positive involvement in society. He trail-blazed a pathway of both intimacy with the Creator and involvement with his creation, and he invited others to follow suit. Even the Essenes, as laudable as their motives may have been, were way off beam as far as living God's way was concerned. In their quest for intimacy with God, they rejected involvement in society and retreated from the public sphere to private isolation. This was not the way of Jesus. His actions sprang from the deep conviction that the One who sent him not only deeply loved the world he had created but was still intimately involved in it, and that only through the engagement of his people in the same task would the longed-for restoration continue. He knew that God's love needed to become visible before it would ever be credible.

> *Jesus' ministry was one multi-faceted response to suffering.*
> David Bosch

Jesus did not bequeath our contemporary Christian dichotomies to us – they came from elsewhere. He never separated the spiritual from the material or the sacred from the secular. Worship was not a thing apart; it was an attitude to the whole of life. For Jesus, worship was about fishing and praying, laughing and meditating, eating and drinking, reading and teaching. And when he challenged people to repent, he meant 'live your life like me, align yourself with my agenda – love God and love your neighbour'. Following Christ was never about merely tipping your cap to some theoretical theological formula only to carry on regardless. It is about being called to a life of intimacy and involvement.

> *Just as in Genesis, so now in the new Genesis, the new creation, God breathes into human nostrils his own breath, and we become living stewards, looking after the garden, shaping God's world as his obedient image-bearers.*
> Tom Wright

More than words

Authentic Christian spirituality has nothing to do with the quest to attain some higher esoteric spiritual experience for the sake of it. In Jesus' thinking, there is no room whatsoever for such escapist, shallow and self-indulgent thinking. Just as his life was about bringing the creator God into the places of poverty, inequality, violence and fear, he implores us to be about this same task (John 17:18). Similarly, just as he brought a deeper understanding of personhood and community, bestowing identity to the marginalized, transforming the consciousness of individuals, families and society as a whole, our calling is to be engaged in the same enterprise. It is the job of the church to interpret Christ to the world by demonstrating the qualities that Jesus demonstrated. If the church loses its hold on its mandate to do this, it quite simply forfeits its right to exist. In our desire to be people of the word, it is easy to become *all words*. As a result, we have often found ourselves silenced and marginalized by the suspicious philosophy of the postmodern world, which says that words don't count for anything. To counter this suspicion, we obviously need more than a new set of words; we need a renewed commitment to a radical theology of incarnation, social engagement and community.

> *The truth of the Christian faith can shine only when it is intelligible through the praxis of Christians.*
> Gerhard Lohfink

Like the ballet dancer who, when asked after her performance what it meant, replied, 'If I could say it, I wouldn't have needed to dance it,' we must be aware of the limitations of words. God, through Jesus, demonstrated his love; he didn't just talk about it. That's what incarnation is all about. It is about vulnerability and genuine engagement. It is about surrendering power and control. It is about leaving the place of safety and heading for the remote, risk-filled but needy outpost (Philippians 2:1ff.). 'To be,' as urban missiologist John U'Ren writes, 'at the coal face of the frontier.' Incarnation is for an 'alien' world. It demands, therefore, that we engage beyond our comfort zones – beyond the limits of our control. Though we should continue to set up our own youth clubs, job clubs, play schemes and IT training centres, etc., our commitment to the doctrine of the incarnation means we should never be satisfied with these. We have a responsibility to get involved, not only with what the church is doing but also with what others are doing. Incarnation requires that we 'play away from home'. We cannot keep ourselves to ourselves. A commitment to the principle of incarnation calls us to a new intimacy and involvement with both God and his creation.

> *I hereby pledge myself – my person and my body – to . . . meditate daily on the teachings and life of Jesus . . . walk and talk in the manner of love, for God is love . . . pray daily to be used by God in order that all men might be free.*
> Pledge signed by civil rights demonstrators,
> Alabama, 1963

Going further

1. The whole lived life of Jesus clearly demonstrates the reality of the kingdom of God. Remembering the phrase 'actions speak louder than words', how are we demonstrating that we live as people of his kingdom?
2. Read Luke 4:14–20, the mission statement of Jesus. What is the mission statement in your work place? What is the mission statement for your church?
3. Jesus called us to love God and love our neighbour as ourself. How should we begin to translate this most important of commands from theory into practice?

4. Through his ministry, Jesus began to re-order society in the way God intended. How can your local church most effectively continue this agenda today?

4. How the West Was Lost: *The Retreat of the Church*

'Your God has had plenty to say to the church in the last few decades, but very little, if anything at all, to say to the nation as a whole,' commented an agnostic contact of mine from one of the national broadsheets. 'He's got a serious case of verbal diarrhoea when it comes to his chosen flock. He just can't stop complimenting you. You're eagles soaring in blue skies, fruitful trees planted by free-flowing rivers and mighty warriors anointed for battle. But when it comes to the rest of society he's been struck dumb. He's lost his nerve or lost his interest.'

Religion and especially Christianity has, in recent times, been the target of much scathing critique and bad press. Exactly how justified many of the accusations are is debatable, but the comments from my journalist friend are, nevertheless, poignant. Even a superficial reading of British history reveals that the church, which once played the most important role in community development and the provision of social welfare, has been sidelined. That many of the once-vibrant parish church buildings located right at the heart of their communities are now decaying and decrepit illustrates the transition well. They tell the story of how an active and involved people became passive and isolated, with an increasingly irrelevant and 'other-worldly' agenda; of how their potent message which once had stinging relevancy and political edge was silenced; of how the West was lost.

Faith in the past

> *Every human society is governed by assumptions normally taken for granted . . . There is no such thing as an ideological vacuum.*
> Lesslie Newbigin

Half a millennium ago, Western Europe was dominated by the Christian faith. The church and its teaching pervaded every aspect of life. God was in his heaven and we, his subjects, were down here on earth to serve his purposes. Monarchs ruled by divine sanction while the populace looked to the provision of a beneficent Creator to bless their toil. The seasons were a gift from the Almighty, and vital to the agricultural foundation on which society was based. He caused the sun to shine, the rain to fall and the crops to grow. Everyone knew that, whatever their station, whether sovereign or serf, all were servants of the one true King of heaven and earth.

This theocentric (God-centred) worldview impacted

every area of life. If you were to ask why some people had power and status and others not, why an apple fell to the ground when the wind tore it from the branch of a tree, or why the sun rose in the morning, most would answer without the slightest hesitation, 'God makes it happen.' Religion, politics and science were one and the same, based on a communal faith interpreted by the church authorities. But ironically, it was the chain of events triggered in the early 1500s by the German monk and father of the Reformation, Martin Luther, that was to change all that for ever.

Until the Reformation, if God was in his heaven then the Pope was his representative on earth and, as such, the Pope's word was law. Now, not only did the Reformation insist on placing the Bible in the hands of the masses but it dared to undermine ecclesial authority further by suggesting that the individual could interpret its teaching independently of Rome. People were encouraged to use their own understanding and powers of reason to arrive at conclusions about life and faith. They were liberated from perceiving themselves as nothing more than passive receivers of the church's dogma to develop their own measuring rods for truth.

All this had huge ramifications for science, which now found itself with a new 'God-given' mandate to seek understanding, free from the shackles of traditional church teaching. Scientists no longer had merely to contemplate the world around them; they could prod and poke it to look for the God behind it – or even question and ultimately reject the notion that there was a creator involved in it at all. So, while the Reformation recovered so much that had been lost to the church, it also had the unexpected legacy of opening the floodgates that were eventually to lead to the collapse of Christendom. The Reformation didn't just reform the church; it was destined to reform society as a whole.

Was the church pushed, or did it jump?

In time, the increasing autonomy of the individual from the governing authority of the church was to become a foundational building block for one of the most influential movements Europe has ever known: the Enlightenment. Carried by their new-found optimism in the ability of the human race to understand and shape the world, the movers and shakers of the Enlightenment began to develop radically new ideas about how the universe worked and the role that God played in it. For instance, one of the Enlightenment's greatest sons, Isaac Newton (1642–1727), famously declared that apples fell as a result of gravity, part of the workings of a rational universe – a universe that scientists increasingly believed they could understand and control. Even though Newton, and others like him, maintained a strong Christian faith, subsequent generations gradually pushed God from his centre-stage position. For them, the very need for a religious, God-centred foundation for society and understanding of the universe was obsolete. And soon the theories of Darwin were to be used to put the final nail in the coffin. His much admired and seminal work, *On the Origin of Species* (1859), allowed people to declare that the idea that human beings are the apex of God's creation was ridiculous. Instead, the human race was merely the most current stage in an on-going evolutionary process; naked apes were no more important than the baboon, and the notion of a creator was absurd.

When Yuri Gagarin returned from his historic space flight in 1961, and proudly declared that he had seen no sign of God up there, that seemed to be a fitting epitaph for any kind of religious worldview. Given the time, money and expertise, nothing now seemed impossible. When scientists could give precise answers to every question, who needed God as a means of explaining things?

John Drane

So it was that the Enlightenment opened up a strange new world where history and faith were no longer perceived as friends but rivals, where facts and values were pushed apart, where religion and politics didn't mix and nature laughed at the notion of super-nature. An anti-religious mood swept through a society that had once furnished its worldview with Christianity. The age of the rationalist materialist had dawned. Science and technology would give humanity the power to fulfil its own destiny. God was relegated to a 'god of the gaps', plugging the holes that this new vision hadn't yet been able to fill – inevitably, an ever-shrinking role.

But the fact is that, as much as the church was pushed in this direction, it was also glad to jump. It willingly retreated from public and corporate life, exiling itself into a ghetto on the margins of society, where it felt safe. Christians appeared happy to teach their kids to sing song lyrics like, 'Jesus bids us shine with a pure, clear light, like a little candle burning in the night. In this world of darkness so we must shine, you in your small corner and I in mine.' The church effectively painted itself into a small corner of existential self-protection, a spiritual realm immune to confirmation or refutation, from where the cry regularly went up: 'The world is welcome to its science and facts. But what's true for me is that God is in my heart.' However, this kind of thinking only served further to hermetically seal off the world of theology and Christian faith from the discoveries of science. The legacy of this dichotomy was brought home to me forcibly when a friend of mine told me of how once he sat in a biology lesson in his secondary school and dared to ask a question about the principles on which what was being expounded was based. He found his inquiring mind was rewarded with a very stern answer: 'Your faith is informing your view of nature. Don't confuse superstition with objective empirical evidence.' Christianity is OK, screams our culture, so long as it remains personal, privatized, experiential and passive, even anti-intellectual.

The slogan that many clergy were taught in seminaries was, 'science tells us how, theology tells us why the world was created.' This is neat, but is basically a schizoid view of reality. The price paid for this uneasy truce with science was the loss of a sense of the whole . . . The earth reveals the glory of God, and scientists uncover God's majesty. Science and religion cannot be separated.

Walter Wink

Faith without God

All this brings us full circle back to a world where faith and religion have no legitimate role to play in modern public life. Religion is OK as long as it's kept 'personal and private' and doesn't interfere with 'real life'. 'Bishops shouldn't meddle in politics; politics and religion don't mix,' they say. In reality, however, the proposal for the separation of faith from the state, or from education and science for that matter, is a misguided and ultimately unachievable goal. The view espoused by secular humanists is no less a faith position than the ones that they so want to see removed from the state. Secular humanism is a religion. And, what's more, it's no less divisive than its competitors. Secular humanists can do just as effective a job when it comes to sectarian intolerance and bigotry as any other fundamentalist. Let no atheist forget the massive human rights abuses of Communist states (e.g. China, the former USSR or Cambodia), engineered by revolutionary Marxism and massacring more people in the last century than all of the other oppressive religions throughout history.

> *The great crisis of humanity today is that it has lost its sense of the invisible. We have become experts in the visible, particularly in the West. If I were called upon to identify briefly the principal trait of the entire twentieth century, I would be unable to find anything more precise and pithy than to repeat again and again, 'Men have forgotten God.' The failings of a human consciousness deprived of its divine dimensions have been a determining factor in all the major crimes of this century.*
> Alexander Solzhenitsyn

Everyone – bar none – lives by faith. Though this may be a difficult concept for a secular humanist to grasp, nonetheless it remains true. Every single person lives by faith, even if it's only faith in themselves or in what they don't believe. Many people are hostile or indifferent to the message of the church because they believe it's subjective, whereas they have their feet firmly on rational ground. However, in reality, this is a viewpoint that has its head in the clouds, unable even to recognize the very basis on which it stands. Christians believe that God is not only present, but involved in the world. They just can't prove it; in the end, it's a statement of faith. Atheists believe that God doesn't exist and so we need to order the world ourselves. But that is equally a faith position. An atheist lives in a world built on faith just as much as a Christian. It's no more 'real' than anyone else's. Therefore, the question isn't whether or not one lives by faith – everyone does! The question is, rather, does your faith work? What does it produce? What difference does it make? How potent or sterile is it?

> *People are what they believe.*
> Anton Chekov

Faith in the future

Whatever happens regarding the future role of traditional, organized religion and its relationship to the state here in the UK, one thing is for certain – the state will still be based on faith. Faith is the only basis for law and morality. Law and morality are about ethics and values. Ethics and values are about philosophy – and philosophy is an issue of faith. Ultimately, a state can choose to ignore organized religion by gradually sidelining it, squeezing it out of political life. But it will still be left to work out its policies, practices and laws based on its values, which can be derived from no other source than its faith position. A secular state may be the dream of many but it will have to answer the same unavoidable question: 'Is our faith worth living by and does it work?'

If that, however, is the challenge that faces secularists, the challenge that faces the church is once again to articulate an integrated, 'joined-up' theology. Our task is to demonstrate unequivocally the holistic approach that the Old Testament expresses and which in the New Testament Jesus declared as the in-breaking kingdom of God. We must, once again, allow our concept of salvation to be shaped by *shalom* – collective and comprehensive well-being – in the here and now, not just beyond the grave.

I spoke recently to a young man who had an unshake-able desire to evangelize the UK. I asked him what his message to the public might be. 'If you die without know-ing Jesus, then you are in big trouble!' was his abrupt reply. I admire his enthusiasm, but what kind of message of hope is that for a single parent struggling to bring up their child on inadequate benefit? What kind of message is that for a busy executive who feels trapped on life's tread-mill with no way off? What kind of message is that for the young teenager who has only known a life of abuse at the hands of their own father? What kind of message is that for the homeless man unwanted by a society driven by 'get' rather than give? It might be a faith to die by but it's not one to live by and, even more importantly, it's not the gospel!

A paradigm shift

It is said that, in hindsight, everyone can see with 20/20 vision. Nowadays, it's easy to see the Enlightenment worldview for what it was in all its naïveté and arrogance. Its heady optimism and proclaimed 'certainties' have long since proved bankrupt – the goods of human progress have not been delivered. Of course, some advances have been made, but the problems loom larger than ever. Consequently, in some circles, there is an insistence that nothing less than another paradigm shift is required. We need to move from an emphasis on rationality, with its tightly sealed compartments which falsely divide reality up into realms of 'public' and 'private', 'faith' and 'facts', 'history' and 'values', to seeing the world as interconnected, holistic and dynamically indivisible. We need an understanding that acknowledges that issues and their solutions are not simply materially but also spiritually generated. The exciting thing is that the Christian faith, once it has been released from the cultural and ideological manacles of the Enlightenment, speaks exactly this language. Rather than being a commodity to be marketed for 'private use only', the gospel becomes an all-embracing truth that challenges the whole of life, both personal and corporate. Christian faith becomes a faith to live by, not just to die by; a faith whose corporate prayer is, 'Our Father . . . Your will be done on earth as it is in heaven.'

A few months ago, I heard Jackie Pullinger speaking at a conference. She said, 'I hear people cry out to the Lord. "More, Lord," they chant. But I wonder what's wrong with them. They must be on the wrong diet. I am satisfied. I am filled. I am content.' Authentic Christian faith, based on intimacy with God and involvement in society, is robust and satisfying. It is a faith that works in the day-to-day reality of life in the twenty-first century. Certainly, New Testament teaching warns us to keep our eyes on the eternal plane, but it never does so at the expense of real engagement in the here and now. As C. S. Lewis put it, we are called to attend to 'eternity itself, and to that point of time which [we] call the present. For the present is the point at which time touches eternity.'

Going further

1. The Reformation and Enlightenment periods saw the Christian church become marginalized and lose its voice in society. If we are confident that the church should be at the centre of our society, how can we go about helping it regain its significance?
2. For many Christians, our relationship with God has become a private affair. What steps can we take that might break through the Christian subculture and allow us to go public once again?
3. Given that everyone lives by faith (faith in themselves, in the teaching of humanism, etc.), how can we be less embarrassed by the concept of faith in God?
4. Often our faith is more dictated to by culture than we realize. The Enlightenment worldview conditioned Christian faith in some very negative ways. How can we monitor our own faith to save it from the same kind of fate in today's world?

5. A Moment of Opportunity:
The Role of the Church in the Twenty-first Century

History records that in Nazi Germany the church failed. Rather than attempting to halt the momentum of Hitler, and in turn the mass genocide of the Jewish people, it either actively sided with his regime or passively accepted it. Dietrich Bonhoeffer, one of the few church leaders who did make a stand against Hitler, and who was imprisoned and later executed as a result, wrote some haunting words on this issue from his death cell. He claimed that because the German church's priority lay in its own self-preservation, it had lost its prophetic role and thus forfeited its opportunity, and indeed God-given responsibility, to speak to humanity.

This same desire for self-preservation was at the heart of the church's weak response in the wake of the Enlightenment – a lack of courage that led not only to its retreat from its divinely appointed role in society but also to its eventual irrelevance. Now, however, is the moment for the church to end this exile, to rediscover its prophetic role and to fulfil its destiny as salt and light.

> *The church must be awakened from the sin of triviality.*
> Reinhold Niebuhr

Seize the day

As the Enlightenment worldview crumbles, optimism is giving way to pessimism, and belief in humanity to suspicion. The West is in the grip of an accelerated cultural transition which is causing social upheaval beyond imagination. Britain, among other nations, is desperately scratching its head trying to find answers to these seemingly interminable problems. This situation, however, has opened the door for clear thinking and fresh vision. Across the UK, there is an openness on the part of both people and government to finding new approaches to intractable problems.

The recognition of the breadth and depth of this need is everywhere. It fills our newspapers and dominates the agendas of our politicians and social commentators. Government speaks of creating well-being in each community, which it defines as physical, social and environmental flourishing; of building active communities and social capital in order to achieve the task; and explicitly of the key role that religious groups have to play in all this.

Here is an opportunity for the church to get involved. For us, terms like 'well-being' have a ring of familiarity about them – an echo of the *shalom* of the Old and New

Testaments. And the truth is that the social reform, so longed for, will never come about exclusively through externals, government programmes or appeals to self-improvement. Society will not thrive and people cannot flourish on mere ideological posturing or hollow encouragement. In the words of the Chief Rabbi:

> *The liberal democracies of the West are ill-equipped to deal*
> *with such problems [poverty, justice and lack of freedom].*
> *That is not because they are heartless but because they have*
> *adopted mechanisms that marginalize moral considerations.*
> *Western politics has become more procedural and managerial.*
>   Jonathan Sacks

As history teaches us, physical provision without spiritual hope is an empty commodity. What is needed is a sense of hope as well as workable holistic solutions. All this adds up to saying that the church has an indispensable role to play in our society. It is time to demonstrate a faith and spirituality that works and delivers.

> *There is a growing recognition that the state can do many*
> *things well, but it cannot deliver the personal or spiritual*
> *support that we all need to overcome life's greatest adversities.*
>   Gary Streeter

Public practice

As an old man, Martin Luther, the father of the Reformation, discussed at length his understanding of the word 'church'. He concluded that it wasn't a private but rather an essentially public phenomenon. Indeed, he states, 'just as public as a town meeting'. He then asks a question: 'How can a poor, confused person tell where this Christian holy people is in the world?' and went on to answer, 'They can tell by its public practices.' Luther's thinking is as relevant today as when he first committed it to paper. It's time once again for the church to go public; to be recognized by our 'public practices' rather than known for our moralistic sermons.

Jesus was a public figure and a prophet. He didn't come with a privatized faith for a few individuals, but an agenda for the whole of Israel. And in the classic tradition of the Old Testament prophets, it was the things he did as much as the things he said that made their impact: he healed the sick; he touched the untouchable; he ate and drank with the undesirable; he associated with the unacceptable; he cleansed the Temple by smashing the tables of the money changers; he died a criminal's death and he rose from the dead. Jesus did extraordinary things – things which made people sit up and take note. His actions ignited debate, created discussion and made everyone think, re-evaluate and often change their opinions, attitudes, values and worldview.

> *We have reduced Christianity into a religion that brings*
> *people to use the right language and to use the right words*
> *instead of compassionately identifying with people's needs. We*
> *have made Christianity into a lifestyle of middle-class*
> *propriety instead of a call to have one's heart broken by the*
> *things that break the heart of Jesus.*
>
> Tony Campolo

Just as Jesus interacted and engaged with his society, if we are to express the message of the kingdom today, then we need to grapple with the issues that are our equivalents of those he saw fit to address. For instance, poverty – we have to redefine the current narrow definition of this term, because as we have seen, for Jesus it encompassed needs much wider than those financial. We will want to ask: Who today are the equivalent of the outsiders, the excluded and the disenfranchised of Jesus' day? Who are the twenty-first century's impure and unclean? Who are Britain's humiliated, marginalized, downtrodden and hopeless? If we are silent on any of these issues we turn our backs on Christ, deny God his rightful place in society and in doing so fall far short of authentic Christian spirituality. More than that, we deny those affected by these issues the hope of God's justice, as well as rob ourselves of the moment of opportunity.

If we are to say that religion cannot be concerned with politics,
then we are really saying that there is a substantial part of
human life in which God's will does not run. If it is not God's,
then whose is it?

Desmond Tutu

Both/and not either/or

However, Jesus did not simply address the needs of individuals; he possessed a deep understanding of the root problems and fearlessly spoke out against the controlling social, economic and political powers. The theologian Walter Wink notes, 'Our task is to work to change structures as well as individuals.' It isn't a question of either/or. It has to be a case of both/and.

This is, as we have seen, one of the hallmarks of faith shown in both the Old and New Testaments – it has just as much to say to society as a whole as it does to individuals; just as much to say about the system as it does about people. For example, in emptying the Temple of merchants, challenging creditors to release clients from debt and rebuking social and religious leaders, Jesus was conducting scathing critiques of the corrupt structures that undergirded his society. Oppressive hierarchies and classism needed to be replaced by justice and social equality; the accumulation of wealth on the part of the few needed to be replaced by a system promoting economic equity; and relationship with the Creator God was not to be limited or regulated by the religiously and socially self-righteous, but was to be open to all, bar none. These values, Jesus' values, must be the values that the church, as the prime agent of God's kingdom, exemplifies today.

Our challenge is not to be overtaken by notions of revival, nor overwhelmed by a struggle for survival. It is to keep our eye firmly on God's enduring agenda: the transformation of our society.
Joel Edwards

Let's get pragmatic

Five years after becoming an MP in 1780 at the age of 21, William Wilberforce became a committed Christian. For a while he considered abandoning his political career in favour of working as a missionary or a minister, but he changed his mind as he began to see the impact he could make through political action. In 1787, he started a lifelong campaign against slavery and a vast range of other social problems, by promoting Bible knowledge and keeping Sunday 'holy', preventing cruelty to children or animals and eradicating poverty. With a complex web of joined-up strategies and a broad spectrum of working partnerships, both religious and political, he laboured tirelessly to turn his dream into reality.

Wilberforce and his friends (later known as the Clapham Sect) epitomized prayerful, persistent Christian pragmatism. His long fight in Parliament to abolish slavery throughout the British Empire, for example, lasted 38 years, and stopped only when ill health forced him to retire from public office. On the way, he found himself working alongside people with agendas radically different from his own – Quakers, for example, who otherwise saw him as being far too conservative, and the followers of Adam Smith, whose objection to slavery was on the purely economic grounds that its running costs were far too high. Wilberforce's ideals were a major drive for abolition, and he never stopped praying for both supporters and opponents, but without his hard-nosed political realism and his willingness to work alongside those with whom he often clashed in other areas, his plans would have come to nothing. The extent to which he was a catalyst for the abolition of slavery was finally realized when his plans in the form of a bill to abolish slavery passed their third reading in the House of Commons on the 26th July 1833. Three days later 'Wilber', as he was known by family and friends, the champion of slaves, died. (For more on Wilberforce, read John Pollock's biography, *Wilberforce: God's Statesman*.)

The Clapham Sect's example is one that is worth copying – praying effectively *for* and engaging effectively *with* government, businesses and others as valued, strategic partners. We don't have to agree totally with everyone we work with, any more than they have to agree with us point for point on our approach. But, as Wilberforce learned, the ability to compromise over non-essentials in the short term is a key component in every successful working relationship.

It seems that the impetus of the incarnation has been lost somewhere in the historical development of the church. Instead of being made present in human life, the God of the church has become remote and thus irrelevant.
Mike Riddell

In fact, of course, it cuts both ways. The more we can learn to accept people and work with them on their own terms, the more credibility and leverage we'll have as we ask that they accept and work with us on our own terms.

One of the distinguishing marks of any Christian organization, from local churches to charities, is our commitment to prayer. Without this, we lose one of the main planks of our identity as a specifically Christian agency, not to mention a key element in our effectiveness. It's not something we impose on others – insisting that our meetings with council officials begin with five minutes of head-down, eyes-closed fervent intercession – but we are committed to intimacy as well as involvement, recognizing that they fuel and sustain one another. We know that it is essential for us, helping us to become more focused, more committed, more enthusiastic and more in tune with God and one another.

So when statutory bodies refuse to respect our right to pray, or discriminate against us under the guise of 'equal opportunities' because we insist that prayer is an integral part of what we do, they act unfairly. And when they refuse to work with us because we're Christian, they act irresponsibly – especially in view of their mandate to provide the kind of best quality, cost-effective care we can help them with. But, by the same token, we act unfairly and irresponsibly when we refuse to work with them because they don't pray or aren't Christian. We may not feel completely comfortable with their values, any more than they do with our faith and prayer, but we're foolish and hypocritical if we let that stand in the way of the kind of pragmatic partnership that can get the job done.

When I was a minister in Tonbridge, the church and the local social services pioneered a very effective strategic partnership – a kind of job-share. One of the church members, Barry, was a qualified and highly experienced social worker, and the church and council agreed to a joint-funding arrangement by which he worked in the church's specific geographical 'patch' under the auspices of both the council and the church. The council recognized that Barry was professional enough not to push his faith on his clients, and that the church respected their position and opinions enough not to encourage him to try. The council also knew that the church offered a unique blend of back-up facilities and inroads into the local community. At the same time, the church recognized that local people had needs that Barry could help meet as a social worker, and that we and the council had a mutual interest in supporting his work.

This is the kind of partnership that we need to be more involved in as local churches and Christian charities. It's the kind of partnership practised by Wilberforce and his colleagues. And it's similar to the kind of pragmatic working arrangement adopted in the Old Testament by characters such as Joseph, Daniel and Nehemiah, who served the pagan kings of Egypt, Babylon, Medea and Persia. Not only should we pray in an informed way for our government, local authorities and other organizations, but as far as we can in all good conscience, we should work alongside them as strategic partners.

> *Perhaps Western culture is nearing a point where the Christian faith can be successfully reintroduced. Maybe the collapse of the present order will lead to a new outbreak of revolutionary Christianity.*
> Howard Snyder

Faith in essence

Being a Christian is not about meeting regularly with like-minded people to sing our favourite songs in a religious social club. Nor is it about badgering people about their eternal destiny whenever half an opportunity rears its head. True Christian spirituality turns on two axes: the first, our relationship with the God of love, generosity and inclusiveness revealed in the person of Jesus Christ, and the second (an inevitable consequence of the first), our love for, and commitment to, others. This necessitates not only an intimacy with God that informs our lives, but a depth of involvement in society that demonstrates the same outrageous love and inclusiveness on which we ourselves are continually dependant. This, and this only, is authentic

Christian spirituality – a faith that works.

> *The way of Christian witness is . . . the way of being in*
> *Christ, in the Spirit, at the place where the world is in pain, so*
> *that the healing love of God may be brought to bear at that*
> *point.*
>
> Tom Wright

Going further

1. Tony Campolo urges us to make Christianity more than 'a lifestyle of middle-class propriety'. How justifiable is his accusation and what can we do about it?

2. We often pray, 'Your kingdom come here on earth, as it is in heaven.' What do we mean by this?

3. In our current culture, there is a strong cry for *shalom* (holistic well-being). What are the ways in which the *shalom* of God might start impacting our friends, family, colleagues and neighbours?

4. The Christian church has, in the past, been more concerned with 'self-preservation' than 'prophetic action'. In what practical ways is your church or can your church begin to reverse that situation?

6. The Faithworks Movement:
How to Get Involved

The Faithworks Movement exists:

- to empower and inspire individual Christians and every local church to develop its role at the hub of the community;
- to challenge and change the public perception of the church by engaging with both media and government.

There is an aching need in every community across the UK – whether rural, suburban or urban – for a fresh approach to tackling besetting needs, and the door of opportunity is wide open for every local church with an appetite to get involved.

But in order to make the biggest impact in our nation, we have to learn to stand and speak together with one voice. On our own we will never be heard. But together it is different. In joining us, by becoming a member of the

Faithworks Movement, you will be declaring to our nation with one voice that faith works! You will be helping in creating a mandate for change, as we endeavour to engage on your behalf with both government and media at a national level.

You can join the Faithworks Movement as an individual, project, church or organization by becoming a member or an affiliate.

Faithworks members

Individuals receive two mailings a year of the Faithworks newspaper giving the latest news, inspirational stories and details of helpful events, resources and contacts on local community action. Members are also offered monthly email news bulletins.

If you believe that faith works, sign up as a member. There is no cost involved, (though a voluntary donation of £5 per year to help us cover our costs would be greatly appreciated).

Faithworks affiliates

Churches, projects or groups of churches can become Faithworks affiliates. In addition to Faithworks newspapers, you receive a specialist newsletter and monthly email bulletin. You also receive free copies of:

- the Faithworks Community Audit
- the Faithworks Church Audit

- the Faithworks Christian Ethos Audit
- a Faithworks Affiliate Certificate

Faithworks affiliates will be asked to pay £20 per year to cover the costs of the packs and mailings.

The principle of professionalism

Adopting a new professionalism is a challenge for us all. We need to demonstrate we are keen to build our capacity and are able to deliver excellent and sustainable, life-changing models of care. Faithworks provides:

Training

• engaging with your community

We provide seminars to help churches begin to unpack issues of social justice, best practice, and ethos and values – how to remain distinctively Christian in a diverse world.

• working with local government

For churches or projects who want to work with local government, these seminars equip churches to make the most of the opportunities available by introducing initiatives such as 'Local Strategic Partnerships' and 'Faith Liaison Officers'.

Clusters

Faithworks is keen to help make connections across the UK, which enable individuals and churches to benefit from each other's experience and expertise.

Faithworks Clusters provide an opportunity for you to share problems and solutions online for the mutual benefit of those engaged in the same area of community work. What do you want to know about – breakfast clubs, youth inclusion, debt advice, crisis pregnancy advice, well-being centres, furniture projects, housing, information centres, sports clubs, gyms . . . etc? Just get in touch.

For more details about membership, affiliation, Clusters and training, visit www.faithworks.info, call 020 7490 9052 or write to:

Faithworks Membership
115 Southwark Bridge Road
London SE1 OAX

Consultants

Our UK team of practitioners are ready to share their expertise and experience with you at every stage as you seek to turn your vision for community engagement into reality. Practical advice and assistance is offered in all areas of community development, including education, finance, strategic planning, management, human resources, health, housing, children's work, youth work, government and social work.

As a church, project or organization you may be just starting out in community engagement or have been running a highly successful community programme for years and be looking for a specialist to advise on building capacity for the future. Whatever your position just get in touch.

Faithworks staff can also offer professional advice on:

- how to turn your vision into reality;
- how to accurately assess your community's needs;
- how to identify and develop your church's resources;
- how to identify and maintain your distinctive Christian ethos in a culturally diverse world;
- how to build strategic partnerships with local government and other agencies.

For more information go online at www.faithworks.info. If you would like some advice or wish to book training or consultancy please contact:

Faithworks Consultancy
115 Southwark Bridge Road
London SE1 0AX
Email: consultancy@faithworks.info
Telephone: 020 7450 9086

Resources

Community Audit

A pack to help you to accurately assess your community's needs.

Church Audit

A pack to help you to identify your church's strengths and weaknesses. This pack can also be used by local Christian organizations or projects.

Christian Ethos Audit

Four packs to help churches, schools and small and large organizations to review and maintain their distinctive Christian ethos in a culturally diverse world.

Different Video

A four-week video teaching programme featuring Steve Chalke, with discussion notes and resources for local churches, cells and other small groups, looking at:

- rediscovering the inclusive and integrated lost message of Jesus;
- developing a distinctive faith in a diverse world;
- integrating intimacy with God with involvement in the community;
- getting beyond the rhetoric to new structures.

Directory of Resources

An online directory of resources from professional agencies, providing helpful information on specific areas of community involvement.

For more information about any of the resources mentioned please go online at www.faithworks.info or call 020 7450 9052.

Aspiring to Excellence

The Faithworks Charter is a 'bench mark' for local churches,

Christian agencies and projects involved in community development work. Please go to www.faithworks.info if you would like to download a copy for discussion with your church, project or organization, with a view to adopting it as an aspirational code of practice to work towards.

THE FAITHWORKS CHARTER

PRINCIPLES FOR CHURCHES AND LOCAL CHRISTIAN AGENCIES COMMITTED TO EXCELLENCE IN COMMUNITY WORK AND SERVICE PROVISION IN THE UK

Motivated by our Christian faith, we commit ourselves to serve others by assuring the following standards are met in all our community work within twelve months of signing this Charter.

Service to the community

1. To serve and to respect all people regardless of their gender, marital status, race, ethnic origin, religion, age, sexual orientation or physical and mental capability.
2. To acknowledge the freedom of people of all faiths or none both to hold and to express their beliefs and convictions respectfully and freely, within the limits of the UK law.
3. Never to impose our Christian faith or belief on others.
4. To develop partnerships with other churches, voluntary groups, statutory agencies and local government wherever appropriate, in order to create an effective, integrated ser-

vice for our clients, avoiding unnecessary duplication of resources.

5. To provide and to publicize regular consultation and reporting forums to client groups and the wider community regarding the effective development and delivery of our work and our responsiveness to their actual needs.

Clients, staff and volunteers

1. To create an environment where clients, volunteers and employees are encouraged and enabled to realize their potential.

2. To assist our clients, volunteers and employees to take responsibility for their own learning and development, both through formal and informal training opportunities and ongoing assessment.

3. To promote the value of a balanced, holistic lifestyle as part of each individual's overall personal development.

4. To abide by the requirements of employment law in the UK and to implement best employment practices and procedures while ensuring that our clients are served by those who share and respect our distinctive ethos and values.

5. To develop an organizational culture in which individuals learn from any mistakes made and where excellence and innovation are encouraged and rewarded.

Management and outcomes

1. To implement a management structure which fosters and

encourages participation by staff at all levels in order to facilitate the fulfilment of the project's goals and visions.

2. Annually to set and to review measurable and timed outcomes, and regularly to evaluate and monitor our management structure and output, recognizing the need for ongoing organizational flexibility, development and good stewardship of resources.

3. To ensure that we are not over-dependent on any one source of funding.

4. To implement best practice procedures in terms of Health and Safety and Child Protection in order to protect our staff, volunteers and clients.

5. To handle our funding in a transparent and accountable way and to give relevant people from outside our organization/ project reasonable access to our accounts.

7. The Faithworks Partners

The Faithworks Movement is built around ten leading Christian organizations that have committed to work together to provide expertise and leadership in the components of effective faith-based community action.

The partners form a high profile, experienced group, capable of challenging and changing the public perception of the church by engaging both media and government and providing key services, tools and resources for churches and their projects as they seek to engage with their local community.

The Faithworks Partners are:
- CARE
- Care for the Family
- Catholic Agency for Social Concern
- *Christian Herald*
- *Christianity+Renewal* magazine
- Credit Action

- Moorlands College
- Oasis Trust
- Shaftesbury Housing Group
- Stewardship Services
- YMCA

CARE

CARE is here to serve, inform and equip you. CARE offers people, ideas, information and resources to churches and individuals who are seeking to be 'salt and light' in their communities.

CARE is a charity that runs projects across the UK, making a tangible Christian difference through networks of volunteers. CARE is active in public life and undertakes practical caring initiatives that affect the lives of thousands. CARE is here to help you be part of the answer.

Caring

- Hospitality network – providing hospitality and refuge, with 350 Christian homes across the UK and a counselling referral service.

- Pregnancy crisis – offering support, advice and information on all options and ongoing practical support, with 150 UK centres.

- Radical care – providing 'for ever families', foster care for young people on remand and befriending adults with learning disabilities.

Campaigning

- Active participation – campaigning across the UK, in Brussels and the UN on issues of human dignity in family, health, education, politics and media.

- Community involvement – training and resourcing Christians to be more effective light and salt, including over 500 school governors and hundreds participating in grassroots politics.

Communicating

- Getting the word out – helping the church to be informed, active and effective with a Christian world-view and publishing specialist research to inform public debate.

- The next generation – shaping education policy, getting resources into thousands of schools, speaking to youth about relationships, facilitating prayer networks for 2,000 schools.

National helplines:

CARELINK – 08457 626 536
Linking you to the care you need via a database of 3,000 specialist agencies in 60 categories.

CARELINE – 0800 028 2228
Providing free, confidential access to advice and counselling on pregnancy and post-abortion care.

CHILDLINK – 0845 601 1134
Helping those helping children, with comprehensive information on childcare issues.

CARE – London, Glasgow, Belfast, Cardiff, Brussels

Head office: 53 Romney Street
London SW1P 3RF
Tel: 0207 233 0455
Email: mail@care.org.uk
Website: www.care.org.uk

Care for the Family

Care for the Family's heart is to strengthen family life and to help those who are hurting because of family trauma.

It is our strong belief that prevention is better than cure, and that's why we put so much effort into events and seminars for those with already good relationships – we want to provide quality input so that they can survive the hard times that usually do come along. Most of our programmes are specifically geared to be available to the whole community – not only the faith groups. They are often publicized by churches who see the value of such programmes to the whole of their community contacts. Previous titles include: *The Sixty-Minute Marriage, Beating Burnout, Maintaining a Healthy Marriage* and *The Heart of a Parent*.

We also have a number of specific programmes that are delivered at a local community level by those in local churches. The Rapport workshops, Developing Closeness in Marriage and Resolving Everyday Issues, are presented to couples all over the country by our trained leaders, often at the request of a 'sponsoring' fellowship. Our new training department will provide materials and support for those who wish to run small groups addressing marriage and parenting issues in their local area on behalf of and for any community group with which they are networked.

Opportunities for new activities are continually being offered and the next year will see an expansion of our work with single parents, step parents, those maturing in years and those parents who have experienced the bereavement of a child. In all these new initiatives, Care for the Family will be partnering with those in churches who can help bring support to their local community.

Care for the Family
PO Box 488
Cardiff CF15 7YY
Tel: 029 2081 1733
Fax: 029 2081 4089
Email: mail@cff.org.uk
Website: www.cff.org.uk

The Catholic Agency for Social Concern

The Catholic Agency for Social Concern is an umbrella body for Catholic charities in England and Wales. It seeks to support, empower and co-ordinate those involved in the reduction of poverty and social exclusion in England and

Wales, and to ensure that the 'option for the poor' is incarnate in the life of the church. CASC is also part of a wider European and international network of Catholic charities.

There are hundreds of Catholic charities in England and Wales, with a combined annual turnover of over £50 million, involving approximately 500,000 staff and volunteers who meet the needs of thousands of individuals, families and communities of all faiths and none.

For more information, to donate or participate, please contact

The Catholic Agency for Social Concern
39 Eccleston Square
London SWIV IBX
Tel: 020 7901 4875

CATHOLIC AGENCY
FOR SOCIAL CONCERN

Christian Herald

As the UK's only interdenominational Christian weekly newspaper, our heartbeat is the local church. Every week, our paper is packed with news of grassroots activity that is making a difference – local churches finding needs to meet, thinking creatively about serving their local community and forging partnerships to improve life for those living around them.

Christian Herald is committed to equipping Christians in a number of ways:

- by helping readers understand the contemporary issues of the day from a biblical standpoint;

- by telling the stories of local churches who are making their presence felt, day by day, in their villages, towns and cities;
- by stretching readers' thinking – stressing that the gospel has something to say and something to do, no matter what the area of contemporary life;
- by providing the information and challenge that can help stir Christians into life wherever God has placed them: work, home, school, neighbourhood.

It's our conviction that for a resurgent church to bring the life and love of Christ to a desperately lost world, it must begin to engage with it sacrificially, humbly and passionately. We hope to help in that process.

Contact details:

Russ Bravo
Editor, Christian Herald
Garcia Estate
Canterbury Road
Worthing
West Sussex BN13 1EH
Tel: 01903 821082
Fax: 01903 821081
Website: www.christianherald.org.uk
Email: editor@christianherald.org.uk

Christianity+Renewal

Christianity+Renewal is a monthly magazine with a readership of over 30,000 who are drawn to its lively mix of news, analysis, columnists, reviews and loads more. Regular contributors include: Tony Campolo, Steve Chalke, Gerald Coates, Jane Collins, Margaret Ellis, Rob Frost, Mark Greene, Joyce Huggett, Jeff Lucas, Mike Pilavachi and Rob Warner.

Christianity+Renewal magazine was launched in 2001 – a merger of two popular and respected titles with their roots in the evangelical and charismatic parts of the church. This 70-plus page magazine aims to reflect its tag line: real life, real faith, in the real world. The readership is drawn from right across the denominations.

A regular article, 'Living churches', features local churches that are making a difference in their local community. Articles identify ideas, principles, programmes and initiatives which other churches can learn from and adapt in their own situation.

Christianity+Renewal encompasses news, culture, reviews, persecuted church news, spirituality, biblical strategies, websites to visit, devotions, insight, leadership issues, theological reflection, true-life ministry stories, plus pages of jobs. Available from all good Christian bookshops or through your letterbox by subscription (saving 30% off the cover price by direct debit). To subscribe phone: 01892 652364 or, for more details, email monarch@premier.org.uk

Christianity+Renewal
Monarch CCP Ltd
PO Box 17911
London SW1E 5ZR
Tel: 020 7316 1450
Fax: 020 7316 1453
Email: monarchccp@premier.org.uk
Website: www.christianityandrenewal.com

Credit Action

Credit Action is a national money education charity, established in 1994. Before becoming an independent charity, it was part of the Jubilee Centre in Cambridge.

Through the media exposure and resources it produces, Credit Action wants to encourage the population at large to have confidence in handling their own money. Major companies, including Boots, NatWest Bank, Sun Life and the Body Shop, have used their materials in the past.

Individuals

Credit Action wants to ensure as many people as possible avoid the pain of debt, by helping them to manage their money more effectively. They produce a range of self-help guides and other publications, aimed at encouraging sensible money management for those currently facing some form of debt, and provide video and study notes for group use in Christian fellowships, though individuals can also benefit from this resource.

Credit Action recognizes that many people who contact

them will already be in some sort of financial difficulty, so they have very close links with the major debt counselling charity, the Consumer Credit Counselling Service. The CCCS provides debt counselling and management services free of charge. Go to www.cccs.co.uk for more information.

Churches

Credit Action also serves local churches by providing a variety of training seminars on the biblical and practical principles of better money management with the aim of helping both congregations and communities in this area.

They speak widely at conferences and other events, providing speakers for local churches when asked, and believe that money and debt advice can be an effective and useful service provided by local churches and other community-based groups.

For further information please contact:

Keith Tondeur,
National Director,
Regent Terrace,
Cambridge,
CB2 1AA
Tel: 01223 324 034
Email: office@creditaction.com
Web: www.creditaction.com

Moorlands College

Moorlands College provides a challenging learning environment where men and women, passionate about Jesus Christ, may be nurtured and equipped to impact both church and world.

As an evangelical, interdenominational Bible college, Moorlands aims for the highest standards in: delivering courses that are biblically based, academically rigorous and culturally relevant; grounding everything in practice to facilitate effective service in today's world and creating a supportive community which promotes spiritual, personal and relational maturity.

In the past decade or so, Moorlands has recognized the crucial nature of understanding what is happening to culture and building courses that equip students to engage relevantly in community work of all types in a professional and biblically coherent fashion.

The formally agreed Aims and Objectives for two of our most popular courses, Community and Family Studies and Youth and Community Work, resonate significantly with the Faithworks goals.

For many years, Moorlands has educated and trained just a select number of students, who, when they graduate, have the learning, the experience and the skills to work with churches, Christian organizations and local authorities in community development work.

Through partnership with Faithworks, Moorlands will now be in a position to share specialist course content and its expertise in training and mentoring with a much wider audience – helping local churches to mobilize their members towards effective community projects.

Moorlands College
Sopley
Christchurch
Dorset BH23 7AT
Tel: 01425 672369
Fax: 01425 674162
Email: Mail@moorlands.ac.uk
Website: www.moorlands.ac.uk

Oasis Trust (founding partner)

Oasis Charitable Trust is an organization committed to demonstrating the Christian faith in action. It works in communities across the world, seeking to provide holistic solutions to the major social issues of our time. Oasis focuses its activities on the poor and marginalized in society and seeks to equip others to engage in similar work to increase the impact of the project in which it gets involved.

Oasis was founded in 1985 by Steve Chalke. It is organized into four major areas of innovative activity:

- *Community action* – working on housing and health care in some of the most vulnerable urban areas, it seeks to teach life skills and break the cycle of no home, no job.

- *Global action* – working directly and with partners in 13 countries around the world, and through the exchange of people, expertise and resources, it seeks to enable churches and communities to empower some of the world's poorest and most marginalized people.

- *Youth action* – investing and training tomorrow's church and community leaders, it also runs social inclusion projects across London, focusing on those at risk of being excluded from the education system.

- *Church action* – equipping the church through personnel, training, consultancy and projects, it also develops new models of culturally appropriate expressions of church for the twenty-first century. Oasis Church Action created Faithworks to enable and inspire every local church to rediscover its role at the hub of the community.

For more information about Oasis, please contact:

The Oasis Centre
115 Southwark Bridge Road
London SE1 0AX
Tel: 020 7450 9000
Fax: 020 7450 9001
Email: enquiries@oasistrust.org
Website: www.oasistrust.org

The Shaftesbury Housing Group

The Shaftesbury Housing Group is a professional charitable

Christian organization established to meet housing and care needs. As at January 2002, the group provides homes and/or care services to over 20,000 people, primarily in the South of England.

Shaftesbury Housing was established by the Shaftesbury Society in 1970 and is now a separate organization. The group's parent association and two of its subsidiaries are registered social landlords – giving access to Housing Corporation funding. The group has a financial turnover of £60 million and employs approximately 1,400 staff.

The group has a wide range of experience in relation to housing and care. This includes major urban regeneration, involving commercial development and training opportunities within multi-cultural communities. Specific examples are the regeneration of 1,000 homes in Hackney and the provision of a community-based housing association for management and improvement of 1,500 homes in Oxfordshire.

The current constituents of the group are:

- Shaftesbury Housing Association – parent association providing family homes and sheltered housing (for rent and leasehold).
- Ashley Homes – residential care and supported housing division.
- Banbury Homes Housing Association – community-based association providing family homes, sheltered housing and some supported housing.
- Kingsmead Homes Ltd – local housing company engaged in urban regeneration, provision of family homes, training and workshop units.

- SOAS Homes Ltd – student housing in London.
- Shaftesbury Student Housing Ltd – student housing and key-worker accommodation.
- Cooper Homes & Developments Ltd – development company.

For further information, please contact:

Clive Bodley
Commercial Director
Shaftesbury Housing Group
1 Mawle Court
Banbury
Oxon OX16 5BH
Tel: 01295 261669
Fax: 01295 265995
Email: cdb@shaftesburyhousing.org.uk
Website: www.shaftesburyhousing.org.uk

Stewardship Services

Stewardship Services is a national Christian charity committed to raising the standard of legal and financial administration in churches and Christian organizations. It provides a range of practical services to help organizations get started as a charity and to meet a number of the ongoing needs and responsibilities that they will face. These include:

Charity formation

Stewardship Services has extensive experience of registering charities and understands the Charity Commission and how to present applications to avoid undue delays. It can set you up with a charitable trust or charitable company specially designed for a church-based charity serving the community.

Payroll administration

Payroll can be a big burden. The service takes care of the details, producing payslips, making payment to the employee's bank account, and dealing with tax and National Insurance.

Employment contract pack

Specially designed for use by a Christian charity, the pack contains a model contract of employment, with a number of variations, and helpful guidance notes.

Gift Aid administration

Outsource tax-effective giving to Stewardship Services and enjoy fast and frequent tax recovery and release from the pressure of meeting Inland Revenue requirements.

Accounts examination service

An independent examination of accounts is a legal requirement when income reaches £10,000 p.a. Stewardship Services is a specialist in this field. Other services include insurance advice and agency, and stewardship consultancy on communicating vision and fundraising.

Service standards and charges

Stewardship Services aims to provide professional quality at reasonable cost. Contact them for details of charges and discounts to Faithworks members.

Contact details:

Stewardship Services
PO Box 99
Loughton
Essex IG10 3QJ
Tel: 020 8502 5600
Fax: 020 8502 5333
Email: info@stewardshipservices.org
Website: www.stewardshipservices.org

YMCA

YMCAs are Christian charities belonging to a national and worldwide movement. YMCAs aim to offer young people and their communities opportunities to develop in mind, body and spirit and so fulfil their potential. Often we work with people at times of greatest need. We believe in:

- personal and social development – so we provide life and job skills training and opportunities for personal growth and challenge;
- nourishing relationships – so we provide parenting programmes and activities which support young people's transition to adulthood;

- strong communities – so we provide housing, community activities and sport, health, exercise and fitness programmes.

Throughout the YMCA we aim to underpin all our work with Christian principles and work for a society where all may flourish. Over 160 YMCAs make up the YMCA movement in England. Each is led by local people for local communities, developing projects to meet identified needs. These local energies are supported by national expertise.

The YMCA, through its local presence, can offer churches and Christian agencies general advice and support based on practical experience in developing and delivering community work and service provision. YMCAs are interested in working in partnership with other organizations who share its ethos and its aims. The YMCA has also developed standards of best practice for many areas of its work, in relation to staff and volunteers, and is willing to discuss how these may be used elsewhere.

Contact details:

YMCA England
640 Forest Road
London E17 3DZ
Tel: 020 8520 5599
Fax: 020 8509 3190
Email: enquiries@ymca.org.uk
Website: www.ymca.org.uk

Faithworks: Stories of Hope

by Steve Chalke and Tom Jackson

Because churches are locally based they respond imaginatively to local needs and issues. No organisation is better placed to deliver the vital practical and spiritual hope which every individual and community needs in order to thrive.

Stories of Hope tells of eight churches from different denominations across the UK who are effectively tackling a wide range of social issues. From debt advice to counselling for domestic violence, from after-school projects to sports clubs, from education to youth work, and from arts initiatives to vocational training – each chapter tells an inspiring story of a local church or individual that has responded to a God-given sense of purpose and direction.

'The stories told in this book are a wonderful inspiration to us all, and speak of the practical hope that the church brings when it is faithful to the call of God. They are an encouragement to us to go and do likewise.'

Sandy Millar
Vicar, Holy Trinity Brompton

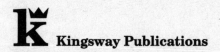 **Kingsway Publications**

Faithworks Unpacked

by Steve Chalke

This manual provides all the information and help you
will need to get involved more effectively in your
local community, and to work with local government
and other agencies to obtain the necessary resources.

*'A comprehensive and practical resource . . . that motivates us to
fulfil our calling.'*

Nicky Gumbel, Alpha and Holy Trinity Brompton

*'A toolkit for every church that wants to roll up its sleeves and get
involved in its community big time.'*

Andy Hawthorne, Founding Director of the Message Trust

*'Provides comprehensive and accessible advice to enable us to build
on this impressive tradition.'*

Sarah Lindsell, Catholic Agency for Social Concern

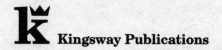

Kingsway Publications